soup &
starter
perfection

HINKLER
BOOKS

soup &
starter
perfection

Food Editor
Jody Vassallo

Creative Director
Sam Grimmer

Project Editor
Lara Morcombe

HINKLER BOOKS

First published in 2004 by Hinkler Books Pty Ltd
17–23 Redwood Drive
Dingley, VIC 3172 Australia
www.hinklerbooks.com

ISBN: 1 86515 768 6
EAN: 9 781865 157689

Printed and bound in China

contents

an introduction to soups and starters

As a savoury entrée or as the centrepiece of a hearty winter's meal, there is nothing as comforting as a bowl of home-made soup. It can be served hot or cold. It can be an elaborate seafood treat brimming with prawns, oysters and fresh herbs or a clever way to resurrect the tired looking vegetables in the refrigerator crisper. It can be a gourmet adventure introducing the international flavours of a Spanish gazpacho, a Vietnamese pho, an Italian minestrone. Or it can be a celebration of simple country-style flavours. Soups are an easy, cheap and versatile meal.

Soups are one way to get a dinner party started. Another is to impress your guests with tasty entrées such as smoked salmon soufflés or grilled oysters with champagne and cream. Cold starters like tricolour canapés or sweet capsicum terrines can be equally impressive. This book contains an array of soups and other hot and cold starters that will complement any meal.

stock

Stocks can either be bought ready-made or made from scratch at home with a minimum of ingredients. If your time is limited there are plenty of good stocks available in supermarkets. Check the labels carefully, however, to avoid soy sauce or other salty flavouring agents.

If you are using a ready-made stock, season your soup only after adding the stock and putting it to the taste test. If you are using powdered stock, keep in mind that they tend to be saltier than liquid stocks.

Freshly made stocks add considerable flavour to soups and if you make them in large batches they can be frozen in airtight containers or in ice-cube trays for later use. With chicken, beef and vegetable stocks, long simmering draws out the flavour of the ingredients, whereas with a fish stock only a little cooking time is required – overcooking can in fact turn the liquid bitter.

The following are recipes for basic stocks:

chicken stock

ingredients

500 g (1 lb) chicken meat and bones
1 onion, chopped
1 carrot, chopped
a handful fresh tarragon, chopped
a handful fresh parsley, chopped
1 bay leaf
salt
1.5 litres (2 ½ pints) water

1 In a saucepan, place the chicken fillets, onion, carrot, herbs and salt. Add hot water just to cover. Bring to a simmer, reduce heat and simmer gently for 1 hour. Turn off heat and cool in its juices. Strain and skim off any fat.

beef stock

ingredients

1 kg (2 lb) shin beef bones
360 g (12 oz) gravy beef
3 litres (5 pints) water
2 carrots, unpeeled and cut into chunks
1 large brown, unpeeled onion, halved
3 medium pieces unpeeled ginger, sliced
1 cinnamon stick
pinch of salt
6 whole cloves
6 peppercorns
6 coriander seeds
4 whole star anise

1 Place water, shin bone and gravy beef in a large pot, bring to the boil, skimming off foam with a large metal spoon. Reduce heat and simmer partially covered for 2 hours, skimming often. Add remaining stock ingredients and simmer for a further 1½ hours. Remove from heat and set aside to cool.

2 Drain and reserve stock through a fine sieve and discard bones, carrots, onion and spices. Skim fat from stock.

fish stock

ingredients

500 g (1 lb) fish pieces and bones
3 sticks celery, roughly chopped
1 carrot, roughly chopped
fresh thyme
1.5 litres (2½ pints) water

1 Into a saucepan, place the fish bones, celery, carrot, thyme and water. Bring to the boil and simmer for 15–20 minutes. Take care not to overcook. Remove from heat and set aside to cool.

2 Drain and reserve stock through a fine sieve and discard bones, celery, carrot and thyme. Skim fat from stock.

vegetable stock

ingredients

1 tablespoon oil
3 sticks celery, chopped
3 cloves garlic, chopped
1 onion, chopped
1 carrot, chopped
1.5 litres (2½ pints) water
a handful fresh thyme
1 bay leaf
¼ teaspoon chilli
salt and pepper

1 In a large heavy-based saucepan, heat the oil on a medium heat. Add the celery, garlic, onion and carrot and cook for 5 minutes. Add the water and bring to the boil. Reduce heat and add the thyme, bay leaf, chilli, salt and pepper. Simmer for 1½–2 hours. Remove from heat and set aside to cool.

2 Drain and reserve stock through a fine sieve and discard celery, carrot, onion and bay leaf.

blending soups

Many of the soups in this book require blending or puréeing after cooking. You can purée soups either in a blender or a food processor. Unless you are using an upright blender, be sure to allow the soup to cool a little before blending or processing. Hot soup in a processor or most blenders could end up all over the kitchen walls and ceiling. The best way to cool soup is to remove it from its cooking pan.

If you are making soups for babies or toddlers, remember to thoroughly check that all the lumps have been removed. Blenders will tend to create a thinner soup than one puréed in a food processor.

storage

Looking for a light lunch or a no-frills Friday evening meal. Easy, defrost and reheat one of the ready-made soups in your freezer. Freezing the leftovers of a huge pot of soup is one of the best things about cooking soups. You can cook as much soup as you like (or your freezer will fit) and none of it needs to be wasted. Most soup will keep in the freezer for 1–3 months or in the refrigerator for up to 3 days.

soups

roasted capsicum and tomato soup

ingredients

3 red capsicums (peppers), halved and deseeded

1 onion, unpeeled and halved

4 large plum tomatoes

4 cloves garlic, unpeeled

1⅓ cups (350 ml, 11 fl oz) chicken or vegetable stock

1 tablespoon tomato purée

salt and black pepper

2 tablespoons chopped fresh parsley

serves 4

preparation time
15 minutes, plus 10 minutes cooling

cooking time
35 minutes

nutritional value per serve
fat: 0.3 g
carbohydrate: 2.7 g
protein: 1.4 g

1 Preheat oven to 200°C (400°F, gas mark 6). Place the capsicums and onion on a baking sheet, cut-side down, add whole tomatoes and garlic. Cook in the oven for 30 minutes or until tender and well browned.

2 Remove from oven and cool for 10 minutes, then peel, discarding skins. Place the vegetables in a food processor with half the stock and process until smooth.

3 Return to the pan, add the remaining stock and tomato purée, stirring to combine, then bring to the boil and cook until heated through. Season to taste and garnish with the parsley just before serving.

tuscan bean and bread soup

ingredients

½ loaf ciabatta
3 tablespoons olive oil
3 onions, chopped
3 cloves garlic, crushed
2 x 400 g (13 oz) cans chopped
  tomatoes
400 g (13 oz) can flageolet beans
2½ cups (600 ml, 1 pint) vegetable stock
salt and black pepper
fresh basil to garnish
serves 4

preparation time
10 minutes
cooking time
20 minutes

**nutritional value
per serve**
fat: 2.8 g
carbohydrate: 13.7 g
protein: 3.5 g

1 Preheat oven to 150°C (300°F, gas mark 2). Cut the bread into small chunks then place on a baking tray in the oven for 10 minutes to dry out.

2 Heat the olive oil in a large pan, add onions and garlic, and cook for 3–4 minutes, until soft. Add tomatoes, beans and stock, bring to the boil, then simmer for 2 minutes.

3 Stir in the diced bread, bring back to the boil, reduce heat then simmer for a further 5 minutes. Season, and serve garnished with basil.

gazpacho

ingredients

2 slices of stale bread (optional)
2 kg (4 lb) tomatoes, chopped
1 cucumber, peeled and chopped
1 green capsicum (pepper), deseeded
    and chopped
1 small onion, chopped
2 cloves garlic, crushed
150 ml (5 fl oz) olive oil
1-2 tablespoons good wine vinegar
    to taste
1 teaspoon cumin seeds or powder
serves 6-8

1 Soak the bread, if using, in a little water. Squeeze out the excess water.

2 Using a food processor or blender, process the vegetables and garlic until well combined, and push through a large sieve into a large bowl.

Use the processor again to process the bread, oil, vinegar and cumin seeds. Add a little water to mixture and add to the bowl of soup. Add a few ice cubes and leave to chill. You can add more water if necessary.

preparation time
10 minutes

cooking time
15 minutes

**nutritional value
per serve**
fat: 5.5 g
carbohydrate: 2.7 g
protein: 1.1 g

parsnip and apple soup with garlic croutons

ingredients

2 tablespoons vegetable oil
1 onion, chopped
2 parsnips, chopped
1 cooking apple, chopped
2$^1/_2$ cups (600 ml, 1 pint) vegetable stock
2 tablespoons chopped fresh parsley
$^1/_2$ teaspoon dried marjoram
1$^3/_4$ cups (440 ml, 14 fl oz) milk
salt and black pepper
extra parsley to garnish
croutons
2 thick slices day-old white bread,
  crusts removed
1 large clove garlic, halved
2 tablespoons vegetable oil
serves 4

preparation time
20 minutes

cooking time
30 minutes

**nutritional value
per serve**
fat: 5.5 g
carbohydrate: 6.2 g
protein: 2.0 g

1 Heat oil in a large heavy-based pan. Add onion and parsnips and cook for 5 minutes or until softened. Add apple, stock, parsley and marjoram and bring to the boil. Cover, reduce heat and simmer for 20 minutes or until the vegetables are tender.

2 Rub both sides of each slice of bread with a half-clove of garlic. Cut the bread into 1 cm cubes. Heat the oil in a heavy-based frying pan. Add the bread and fry for 2–3 minutes, until golden, stirring constantly. Drain on kitchen towels

3 Remove soup from heat. Stir in the milk and season to taste. Blend until smooth in a food processor or with a hand blender. Reheat and serve with the croutons. Garnish with the parsley.

spicy
lentil
soup

ingredients

250 g (8 oz) dried split red lentils
1 litre (1²/₃ pints) good quality
  vegetable stock
1 tablespoon vegetable oil
1 medium onion, finely chopped
1 clove garlic, crushed
2.5 cm knob of ginger, finely grated
2 teaspoons ground cumin
¹/₂ teaspoon cayenne pepper
salt and black pepper
juice of ¹/₂ lemon
serves 4

preparation time
10 minutes

cooking time
45 minutes

**nutritional value
per serve**
fat: 1.9 g
carbohydrate: 7.7 g
protein: 5.2 g

1 Place lentils in a sieve and rinse under cold running water, then place in a large pan. Pour over the stock. Bring to the boil, reduce heat, cover and simmer for 20 minutes.

2 Heat oil in a large frying pan, add onion and cook over a gentle heat, stirring occasionally, for 5 minutes or until softened. Add garlic, ginger, cumin and cayenne pepper and cook for a further minute

3 Add the onion mixture to the lentils, season to taste. Cook for a further 20 minutes, or until lentils are completely soft. Add lemon juice, season to taste and serve.

easy french onion soup

2 Add the flour and cook, stirring constantly for 2–3 minutes. Gradually pour in the stock, stirring constantly and bring to the boil. Reduce heat and simmer, covered for 30 minutes. Season to taste.

3 Preheat grill to high. Toast the french bread on one side then place grated cheese on uncooked side and grill until melted and browned. Pour soup into warmed serving bowls, placing a piece of cheese toast on each.

preparation time
10 minutes

cooking time
1 hour 10 minutes

nutritional value per serve
fat: 3.9 g
carbohydrate: 5.1 g
protein: 2.4 g

ingredients

4 tablespoons butter
750 g (1¹/₂ lb) onions, thinly sliced
1 clove garlic, crushed
2 teaspoons plain flour
1.2 litres (2 pints) good quality beef stock
salt and black pepper
4 slices french bread, about 2.5 cm thick
60 g (2 oz) gruyére cheese, grated
serves 4

1 Heat the butter in a large heavy-based pan over a low heat until melted and foaming. Add onions and garlic, cover, and cook slowly, stirring often, for 30–35 minutes, until onions are golden brown.

provençal-style soup with spring onion pesto

ingredients

2 tablespoons extra virgin olive oil
1 onion, chopped
1 medium potato, peeled and chopped
1 carrot, chopped
1 yellow capsicum (pepper), deseeded and chopped
2 cups (500 ml, 16 fl oz) vegetable stock
2 celery sticks, chopped
2 zucchini (courgettes), chopped
400 g (13 oz) can tomatoes, chopped
1 tablespoon tomato purée
sea salt
freshly ground black pepper

pesto

6 spring onions (green onions), chopped with green part
60 g (2 oz) parmesan cheese, grated
4 tablespoons extra virgin olive oil

serves 4-6

preparation time
20 minutes

cooking time
25 minutes

nutritional value
fat: 7.2 g
carbohydrate: 2.9 g
protein: 2.3 g

1 For the soup, heat oil in a large heavy-based pan, add onion, potato, carrot and capsicum. Cook uncovered for 5 minutes over a medium heat, stirring occasionally, until vegetables begin to brown.

2 Add the stock, celery and zucchini and bring to the boil. Cover, reduce heat and simmer for 10 minutes or until the vegetables are tender. Stir in tomatoes, tomato purée and season generously. Simmer uncovered for 10 minutes.

3 For the pesto: place spring onions, parmesan and oil in a food processor and process to a fairly smooth paste. Ladle soup into bowls and top with a spoonful of pesto.

avocado gazpacho

ingredients

2 large avocados, chopped
grated rind (zest) and juice of 1 lemon
2½ cups (600 ml, 1 pint) vegetable stock
2 large tomatoes
1 cucumber, chopped
1 green capsicum, deseeded and chopped
1 red capsicum, deseeded and chopped
1 clove garlic, crushed
salt and black pepper
4 tablespoons fresh chives, snipped
  to garnish
serves 4

preparation time
15 minutes, plus 1
hour chilling

**nutritional value
per serve**
fat: 5.7 g
carbohydrate: 1.4 g
protein: 0.3 g

1 Place the avocados, lemon rind, lemon juice and stock in a food processor and blend to a thin, smooth purée. Pour into a large bowl and set aside.

2 Place the tomatoes in a bowl, cover with boiling water and leave for 30 seconds. Remove from the bowl, peel, deseed and chop the flesh. Reserve a little chopped tomato and cucumber for the garnish. Place the remaining tomatoes and cucumber in the food processor along with the capsicums, garlic and seasoning, then blend to a purée.

3 Add the tomato mixture to the avocado purée, mixing thoroughly. Cover and refrigerate for 1 hour, then serve garnished with chives and the reserved tomato and cucumber.

spinach and almond soup

ingredients

450 g (14 oz) baby spinach
2 1/2 cups (600 ml, 1 pint) vegetable stock
100 g (3 1/2 oz) ground almonds
salt and black pepper
1/2 cup (125 ml, 4 fl oz) pouring cream
60 g (2 oz) parmesan, grated to serve
serves 4

1 Place spinach in a large pan with stock, reserving a few leaves for garnish. Bring to the boil, reduce heat and simmer for 5 minutes. Stir in the ground almonds and seasoning and simmer for a further 2 minutes. Remove from heat and cool a little.

2 Pour into a food processor and process until smooth. Add the cream, return to the pan and reheat gently – do not boil. Serve topped with parmesan and seasoned with black pepper. Garnish with reserved spinach leaves.

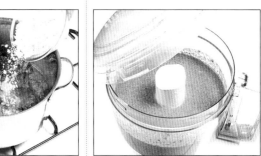

preparation time
5 minutes

cooking time
15 minutes

nutritional value per serve
fat: 9.8 g
carbohydrate: 1.2 g
protein: 4.7 g

sweet potato and rosemary soup

ingredients

3 tablespoons olive oil
2 cloves garlic, crushed
1 medium onion, chopped
1 tablespoon fresh chopped rosemary
2 tablespoons tomato pesto
1 medium carrot, diced
1 large potato, diced
750 g (1½ lb) sweet potato
1 litre (1⅔ pints) chicken stock
freshly ground pepper and salt
extra 2 tablespoons fresh chopped
  rosemary
serves 4-6

1 Heat oil in a large pan, add the garlic, onion and rosemary, and cook on medium heat for 3–5 minutes, or until soft.

2 Add the tomato pesto, and cook, for a further minute.

3 Add carrot, potato and sweet potato, and cook a further 5 minutes. Add the chicken stock and pepper and salt, bring to boil, reduce the heat, and simmer covered for 30–40 minutes, or until vegetables are soft.

4 Purée the soup in a food processor in batches, return soup to pan, add the extra rosemary, and gently heat through before serving. Add extra stock if soup is too thick.

preparation time
20 minutes

cooking time
45 minutes

nutritional value per serve
fat: 3.9 g
carbohydrate: 6.6 g
protein: 1.6 g

mixed vegetable and bean soup

ingredients

2 tablespoons olive oil
1 onion, finely chopped
2 cloves garlic, crushed
1 potato, finely diced
1 carrot, finely diced
2 teaspoons cumin seeds
900 ml (1½ pints) vegetable stock
2 sticks celery, finely chopped
1 large zucchini (courgette), finely
   chopped
125 g (4 oz) fine green beans, cut into
   2.5 cm pieces
425 g (14 oz) can butter beans, drained
400 g (13 oz) can tomatoes, chopped
black pepper
60 g (2 oz) cheddar cheese, grated
serves 4

1 Heat oil in a large heavy-based pan, add onion, garlic, potato, carrot and cumin seeds. Cook, uncovered, for 5 minutes, stirring occasionally, until the vegetables have softened.

2 Add the stock, celery and zucchini and bring to the boil. Cover and simmer for 10 minutes or until the celery and zucchini are tender.

3 Stir in beans, butter beans, tomatoes and season to taste. Simmer, uncovered, for 5 minutes or until the beans are tender. Pour soup into bowls and top with cheese.

preparation time
15 minutes

cooking time
25 minutes

**nutritional value
per serve**
fat: 2.5 g
carbohydrate: 2.5 g
protein: 1.9 g

cream of mushroom soup with crispy onions

ingredients

2 tablespoons butter
1 tablespoon extra virgin olive oil
4 spring onions (green onions), chopped
400 g (13 oz) mushrooms, chopped
1 medium potato, peeled and chopped
900 ml (1½ pints) vegetable stock
sea salt
freshly ground black pepper
4 tablespoons thick cream
juice of ½ lemon
chopped fresh parsley
crispy onions
sunflower oil
1 large onion, finely sliced into rings
1 tablespoon plain flour
serves 4

1 Heat butter and oil in a large pan and fry the spring onions and mushrooms over a medium-high heat for 5 minutes, until softened.

preparation time
15 minutes

cooking time
30 minutes

nutritional value
fat: 5.5 g
carbohydrate: 2.9 g
protein: 1.9 g

2 Add the potato, vegetable stock and seasoning and bring to the boil. Reduce heat, cover and simmer for 20 minutes until the potatoes are tender. Allow to cool.

3 For the onions, heat about 1 cm oil in a large frying pan. Coat onions in the flour, add to the pan and cook for 5 minutes or until crisp and lightly golden. Drain on kitchen paper.

4 Purée the soup in a food processor and return to the pan, stir in the cream and lemon juice and gently reheat. Ladle the soup into bowls and top with the crispy onions. Sprinkle with chopped fresh parsley, to garnish.

chicken and leek soup with herb dumplings

ingredients

4 chicken thighs on the bone, about
    800 g (1 lb 10 oz)
1 onion, chopped
1 carrot, chopped
herb bundle made up of fresh tarragon,
    parsley and a bay leaf
4 tablespoons butter
300 g (10 oz) potatoes, cubed
3 large leeks, sliced
salt and black pepper
2 chicken breast fillets, about 500 g
    (1 lb), cut into small strips
2 teaspoons chopped fresh tarragon
150 ml (5 fl oz) pouring cream
dumplings
100 g (3½ oz) self-raising flour
30 g (1 oz) fresh white breadcrumbs
60 g (2 oz) shredded suet
3 tablespoons chopped fresh herbs
    (tarragon, parsley or chives)
serves 4

preparation time
25 minutes

cooking time
1 hour 45 minutes

nutritional value
fat: 11.5 g
carbohydrate: 7.5 g
protein: 10.8 g

1 Place the chicken–thighs, onion, carrot and herbs in a large pan with 1.5 litres (2½ pints) of water. Simmer, covered, for 1 hour. Strain the stock and skim off any fat. Finely chop the chicken, discarding the skin and bones. Heat half the butter in a separate large pan. Add the potatoes and ⅔ of the leeks, cover and cook for 10 minutes. Pour in 1 litre (1⅔ pints) of the stock and season. Simmer for 10–15 minutes, until softened. Blend until smooth in a food processor, return to the pan, then stir in the cooked chicken. Set aside, keep warm.

2 To make the dumplings, combine flour, breadcrumbs, suet, herbs and seasoning in a large bowl. Stir in 4 tablespoons of water, mix well to combine, then shape into 8 dumplings. Cook in simmering salted water for 15–20 minutes.

3 Heat the remaining butter in a large frying pan. Cook the chicken breast for 4–5 minutes on each side. Add the remaining leek and cook for 2–3 minutes, until tender, then add to the soup with the tarragon and more stock, if necessary. Bring to the boil and simmer for 2 minutes. Remove from the heat and stir in the cream. Divide between 4 serving bowls. Drain the dumplings and add 2 to each bowl.

indian-curried vegetable soup

ingredients

2 tablespoons butter or ghee
2 teaspoons turmeric
4 cloves garlic, crushed
1 tablespoon mild curry powder
1 tablespoon garam masala
1 tablespoon finely chopped ginger
1 teaspoon chilli flakes
4 medium potatoes, peeled and chopped
2 sweet potatoes, peeled and chopped
2 turnips, peeled and chopped
1 parsnip, peeled and chopped
4 medium carrots, peeled and chopped
1 medium butternut pumpkin, peeled
   and chopped
1 litre (1 ²/₃ pints) vegetable stock
1 ²/₃ cups (400 ml, 13 fl oz) coconut milk
4 medium zucchini (courgettes), sliced
400 g (13 oz) peas, shelled
salt and pepper to taste
30 g (1 oz) coriander leaves
serves 4-6

preparation time
30 minutes

cooking time
1 hour 10 minutes

**nutritional value
per serve**
fat: 2.8 g
carbohydrate: 5.9 g
protein: 2.0 g

1 Heat the ghee or butter in a large pan. Add turmeric, garlic, curry powder, garam masala, ginger and chilli flakes and sauté until fragrant.

2 Add potatoes, sweet potatoes, turnips, parsnips, carrots and pumpkin to the spice mixture along with the stock and bring to the boil. Reduce heat and simmer for 45 minutes until the vegetables are tender.

3 Add the coconut milk, zucchini and peas and continue to simmer for 15 minutes.

4 Season to taste and serve garnished with coriander.

cool cumin-scented yoghurt soup

ingredients

1 teaspoon cumin seeds
1 teaspoon nigella (black onion) seeds
1 tablespoon ghee or butter
4 spring onions (green onions),
   finely sliced
10 fresh mint leaves
2 teaspoons ground cumin
1 teaspoon turmeric
60 g (2 oz) cashew nuts
300 g (10 oz) can chickpeas, drained
   and rinsed
2 cups (500 g, 1 lb) natural yoghurt
200 ml (7 fl oz) sour cream
200 ml (7 fl oz) water
salt and pepper to taste
600 g (1¼ lb) cucumbers
1 tablespoon sugar
2 tablespoons shredded coconut,
   toasted
mint leaves for garnish

serves 6

1 Heat a large frying pan and add the cumin and nigella seeds. Toss around the dry hot pan for 3 minutes until seeds are fragrant and beginning to pop. Remove seeds and set aside.

2 Add ghee or butter to the pan and add spring onions and mint leaves and sauté on a medium-high heat for a few minutes until spring onions have wilted. Add ground cumin, turmeric and cashew nuts and toss until the spices are fragrant and the nuts are golden. Add chickpeas and cook for a further 2 minutes. Set aside.

3 In a large bowl, whisk together the yoghurt, sour cream and water until smooth. Season to taste. Peel the cucumbers and scrape out the seeds. Cut the cucumber flesh into thin slices and add to the yoghurt mixture.

4 Add sugar and the spring onion and spice mixture to the yoghurt and stir thoroughly to combine. Allow to stand for 1 hour before serving. Garnish with toasted coconut, sliced mint leaves and a few nigella seeds.

preparation time
20 minutes

cooking time
20 minutes, plus
1 hour standing

**nutritional value
per serve**
fat: 8.8 g
carbohydrate: 6.4 g
protein: 3.5 g

mixed bean soup

ingredients

90 g (3 oz) dried red kidney beans
90 g (3 oz) dried cannellini beans
2 tablespoons olive oil
60 g (2 oz) bacon, chopped
1 onion, chopped
1 clove garlic, crushed
3 stalks celery, sliced
2 carrots, chopped
2 potatoes, chopped
1.5 litres (2$\frac{1}{2}$ pints) chicken or
  vegetable stock
440 g (14 oz) can crushed tomatoes
$\frac{1}{2}$ cabbage, finely shredded
4 tablespoons small pasta shapes or rice
1 teaspoon dried mixed herbs
freshly ground black pepper
parmesan cheese, grated

serves 4

1 In a large bowl, place red kidney and cannellini beans. Cover with cold water and set aside to soak overnight. Drain.

2 Heat oil in a large pan over a medium heat, add bacon, onion and garlic and cook, stirring, for 5 minutes or until onion is tender. Add celery, carrots and potatoes and cook for a further minute.

3 Stir in stock, tomatoes, cabbage, pasta or rice, red kidney and cannellini beans, herbs and black pepper to taste and bring to the boil. Boil for 10 minutes, then reduce heat and simmer, stirring occasionally, for 1 hour or until beans are tender. Sprinkle with parmesan cheese and serve.

preparation time
20 minutes, plus
overnight cooking

cooking time
1 hour 15 minutes

**nutritional value
per serve**
fat: 1.9 g
carbohydrate: 6 g
protein: 2.2 g

indian-spiced potato and onion soup

ingredients

1 tablespoon vegetable oil
1 onion, finely chopped
1 cm piece fresh root ginger, finely chopped
2 large potatoes, cut into 1 cm cubes
2 teaspoons ground cumin
2 teaspoons ground coriander
1/2 teaspoon turmeric
1 teaspoon ground cinnamon
1 litre (1²/₃ pints) chicken stock
salt and black pepper
1 tablespoon natural yoghurt to garnish
serves 4

1 Heat the oil in a large saucepan. Fry onion and ginger on a medium heat for 5 minutes or until softened. Add potatoes and fry for a further minute, stirring often.

2 In a small bowl combine the cumin, coriander, turmeric and cinnamon with 2 tablespoons of cold water to make a paste. Add to the onion and potato, stirring well, and fry for 1 minute or until fragrant.

3 Add the chicken stock and season to taste. Bring to the boil, reduce heat, cover and simmer for 30 minutes or until the potato is tender. Blend until smooth in a food processor or press through a metal sieve. Return to the pan and gently heat through. Garnish with the yoghurt and extra black pepper.

preparation time
10 minutes

cooking time
40 minutes

nutritional value per serve
fat: 1.7 g
carbohydrate: 3.4 g
protein: 1.4 g

minestrone soup with soda bread

and milk and stir into the flour mixture to form a soft but not sticky dough.

2 Knead the dough lightly on a floured surface and flatten slightly into a 20 cm round. Place on a baking sheet and cut a cross into the top. Cook at the top of the oven for 35–40 minutes, until well risen and golden.

3 Heat oil in a large pan. Add the bacon, onion, garlic, carrot, leek and potato and cook for 5–10 minutes or until softened. Pour in the stock and tomato purée, then simmer, covered, for 20 minutes or until vegetables are tender. Break the spaghetti into 2.5 cm lengths and add to the pan. Cook for 10 minutes or until the pasta is al dente. Season to taste and serve with the bread.

ingredients

1 tablespoon vegetable oil
6 rashers rindless streaky bacon, chopped
1 onion, chopped
2 cloves garlic, chopped
1 carrot, diced
1 leek, diced
1 small potato, diced
1.2 litres (2 pints) vegetable stock
2 tablespoons tomato purée
60 g (2 oz) dried spaghetti
salt and black pepper
soda bread
250 g (8 oz) wholemeal flour
250 g (8 oz) plain flour
$\frac{1}{2}$ teaspoon salt
1 teaspoon bicarbonate of soda
4 tablespoons chilled butter, cubed
2 tablespoons chopped fresh parsley
juice of $\frac{1}{2}$ lemon
1 cup (250 ml, 8 fl oz) milk
serves 4

1 Preheat the oven to 200°C (400° F, gas mark 6). To make the bread, place the wholemeal flour into a large bowl, then sift in the plain flour, salt and bicarbonate of soda, mixing well. Rub in the butter, using fingertips until mixture resembles coarse breadcrumbs. Mix in the parsley. Combine lemon juice

preparation time
30 minutes

cooking time
40 minutes

nutritional value per serve
fat: 11.5 g
carbohydrate: 14.9 g
protein: 5.2 g

beef pho

ingredients

stock

1 kg (2 lb) shin beef bones
360 g (12 oz) gravy beef
3 litres (5 pints) water
2 carrots, unpeeled and cut into chunks
1 large brown, unpeeled onion, halved
3 medium pieces unpeeled ginger, sliced
1 cinnamon stick
pinch of salt
6 whole cloves
6 peppercorns
6 coriander seeds
4 whole star anise

soup

250 g (8 oz) thick fillet steak in one piece
500 g (1 lb) flat, thick, dried noodles
2 tablespoons fish sauce
1 brown onion, thinly sliced into rings
3 spring onions (green onions), finely chopped
45 g (1½ oz) bean shoots
15 g (½ oz) fresh coriander sprigs
25 g (¾ oz) mint leaves, chopped
1 small red chilli, deseeded and sliced into rings

serves 8-10

preparation time
30 minutes

cooking time
1 hour 50 minutes

nutritional value
fat: 11.6 g
carbohydrate: 14.8 g
protein: 1.4 g

1 Place water, shin bone and gravy beef in a large pot, bring to the boil, skimming off foam with a large metal spoon.

Reduce heat and simmer partially covered for two hours, skimming often. Add remaining stock ingredients and simmer for a further 90 minutes. Remove from heat, set aside to cool.

2 Drain and reserve stock through a fine sieve and discard bones, carrots, onion and spices. Skim fat from stock. Cut gravy beef finely across the grain. Slice raw fillet steak to paper thinness. Set aside.

3 Soak rice noodles in warm water about 20 minutes until soft, drain and reserve.

4 Return stock pot to heat to boil with fish sauce then reduce heat to very low.

5 Serve boiling stock first then drained noodles into 6 bowls, top equally with shin meat, raw onion rings, spring onions, raw fillet steak slices, which will par-cook in the bowls, and garnish with coriander, mint and chilli.

manhattan oyster chowder

ingredients

2 tablespoons olive oil
1 onion, roughly chopped
125 g (4 oz) mushrooms, quartered
2 cloves garlic, crushed
3 cups (750 ml, 1$^{1}/_{4}$ pints) fish stock
470 g (15 oz) can tomatoes, seeded and
    chopped (liquid reserved)
1 bay leaf
$^{1}/_{2}$ teaspoon dried rosemary
$^{1}/_{2}$ teaspoon dried oregano
pinch hot pepper flakes
1 zucchini (courgette), roughly chopped
600 ml (1 pint) bottled oysters
fresh parsley to garnish

serves 6

preparation time
20 minutes

cooking time
40 minutes

**nutritional value
per serve**
fat: 3.2 g
carbohydrate: 1.7 g
protein: 6.2 g

1 Heat the oil in a large pan and saute the onions and mushrooms over a high heat, until golden. Add garlic and cook stirring for 1 minute. Add fish stock, chopped tomatoes and the reserved liquid. Stir in bay leaf, rosemary, oregano, and hot peppers. Bring to a boil, reduce heat and simmer, partially covered, for 25 minutes.

2 Add zucchini chunks, cover, and simmer for a further 10 minutes, until the zucchini is almost tender. Then slip the oysters with their liquid into the soup and cook, uncovered, just until their edges begin to curl. You want them tender, not chewy.

3 Ladle immediately into bowls. Sprinkle with parsley and serve immediately.

creamy lobster chowder

ingredients

370 g (12 oz) lobster meat, diced
4 tablespoons quick cooking rice
1 teaspoon salt
$1/4$ teaspoon pepper
$1/4$ teaspoon dried paprika
1 tablespoon onion, finely diced
1 small red capsicum (pepper), diced
2 stalks celery, chopped
2 cups (500 ml, 16 fl oz) milk
2 cups (500 ml, 16 fl oz) single cream
2 tablespoons butter
2 tablespoons chopped fresh parsley
serves 4-6

1 Combine rice, salt, pepper, paprika, onion, capsicum, celery, milk and cream in a large pan. Cook over medium heat, stirring frequently, for 10–12 minutes, or until the rice softens.

2 Stir in the lobster and butter. Remove from heat, add parsley, stir to combine and serve.

preparation time
15 minutes

cooking time
15 minutes

nutritional value per serve
fat: 15.9 g
carbohydrate: 5.8 g
protein: 6.8 g

creamy oyster bisque

ingredients

20 fresh oysters, shucked
low-salt fish or vegetable stock
1/2 cup (125 ml, 4 fl oz) white wine
1 small white onion, diced
1 stalk celery, diced
400 g (13 oz) potato, peeled and diced
1 tablespoon chopped fresh thyme
1/2 cup (125 ml, 4 fl oz) low-fat milk
freshly ground black pepper
sprigs watercress or fresh parsley,
  optional
serves 4

ingredients

20 fresh oysters, shucked
low-salt fish or vegetable stock
1/2 cup (125 ml, 4 fl oz) white wine
1 small white onion, diced
1 stalk celery, diced
400 g (13 oz) potato, peeled and diced
1 tablespoon chopped fresh thyme
1/2 cup (125 ml, 4 fl oz) low-fat milk
freshly ground black pepper
sprigs watercress or fresh parsley,
  optional
serves 4

preparation time
20 minutes
cooking time
25 minutes

nutritional value
fat: 0.7 g
carbohydrate: 5.4 g
protein: 4.4 g

1 Pour any liquid from the oysters into a cup. Add enough stock to make up to 1 cup (250 ml, 8 fl oz).

2 Heat 2 tablespoons of the wine in a large pan over a low heat. Add onion and celery. Cook, stirring, for 4–5 minutes or until onion is transparent. Add potato and thyme. Stir in stock mixture and remaining wine. Bring to the boil. Reduce heat and simmer for 10–15 minutes or until potatoes are tender and most of the liquid is absorbed. Cool slightly.

3 Transfer mixture to a food processor or blender. Add half the oysters, the milk and black pepper to taste. Purée. Return mixture to a clean pan. Bring to the boil. Remove soup from heat. Stir in remaining oysters.

4 To serve, ladle soup into warm bowls and top with watercress sprigs or parsley, if desired.

salmon and rice noodles in coconut soup

ingredients

2 stalks lemon grass
2 cloves garlic, crushed
1 large onion, chopped
1 teaspoon ground turmeric
1 teaspoon ground hot chilli powder
1 tablespoon vegetable oil
400 ml (13 fl oz) can coconut milk
1¼ cups (315 ml, 10 fl oz) fish or
   chicken stock
250 g (8 oz) skinless salmon fillet,
   cut into 2.5 cm cubes
salt
125 g (4 oz) dried rice noodles
200 g (7 oz) fresh bean shoots
fresh coriander to garnish
1 lime, quartered, to serve

serves 4

preparation time
25 minutes

cooking time
30 minutes

**nutritional value
per serve**
fat: 8.1 g
carbohydrate: 3.9 g
protein: 4.5 g

1 Peel the outer layers from the lemon grass stalks and finely chop the lower white bulbous parts, discarding the fibrous tops. Place lemon grass, garlic, onion, turmeric and chilli powder in a blender and process to a coarse paste or grind with a pestle and mortar.

2 Heat the oil in a large, heavy-based pan. Fry the paste for 5 minutes until fragrant, stirring often. Add the coconut milk and stock, bring to the boil, stirring, reduce heat, cover and simmer for 15 minutes. Add the salmon and salt to taste, then simmer, covered, for 5 minutes or until fish has cooked through.

3 Cook noodles in a large pan of boiling water until al dente. Rinse well under cold water. Divide rice noodles and bean shoots between serving bowls and ladle over the salmon and coconut soup. Garnish with coriander and lime wedges.

hot-and-sour scallop soup

ingredients

1 litre (1²/₃ pints) chicken broth
125 g (4 oz) mushrooms, thinly sliced
60 g (2 oz) bamboo shoots, sliced
250 g (8 oz) sea or bay scallops, sliced
   5 mm thick
1 teaspoon soy sauce
¼ teaspoon white pepper
2 tablespoons cornflour
3 tablespoons warm water
1 egg, beaten
3 tablespoons rice vinegar
2 spring onions (green onions), thinly
   sliced

serves 4

1 Place chicken broth, mushrooms and bamboo shoots in a large pan. Bring to the boil, reduce heat and simmer 5 minutes. Rinse scallops under cold running water. Add scallops, soy sauce and pepper to the pan. Bring to the boil.

2 Combine cornflour and warm water. Add to the soup and stir until thickened. Stir briskly with a chopstick whilst gradually pouring in egg. Remove from heat. Stir in rice vinegar (white-wine vinegar may be substituted); sprinkle with spring onions. Serve immediately.

preparation time
20 minutes

cooking time
25 minutes

nutritional value per serve
fat: 0.8 g
carbohydrate: 2.6 g
protein: 3.4 g

starters
cold

tricolore canapés

ingredients

tomato toasts
3 slices thick-cut sandwich loaf
1 clove garlic, crushed
3 tablespoons olive oil
2 tablespoons pesto
150 g (9 oz) mozzarella cheese, cut into
   12 slices
3 small tomatoes, thinly sliced and ends
   discarded
12 small pitted black olives

salmon rounds
4 slices dark or light rye bread
1 tablespoon butter, softened
150 g (5 oz) smoked salmon, cut into
   ribbons
2 teaspoons lemon juice
3 tablespoons fromage frais
1 teaspoon horseradish cream

cucumber bowls
1 cucumber
100 g (3½ oz) cream cheese
1 tablespoon chopped fresh tarragon
salt and black pepper

serves 6

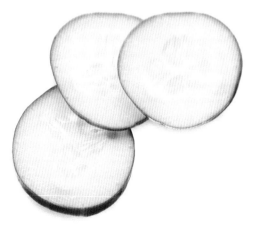

preparation time
15 minutes

cooking time
6 minutes

**nutritional value
per serve**
fat: 12.2 g
carbohydrate: 10 g
protein: 8 g

1 Refrigerate sandwich and rye breads for 2 hours.

2 Make the cucumber bowls: Peel strips of skin from the length of the cucumber to give a striped effect and cut into 1 cm thick rounds. Using a teaspoon, remove some seeds from each round to make a hollow. Pat dry. In a small bowl combine cream cheese, tarragon, salt and pepper. Fill cucumber hollows with cream cheese mixture, season with black pepper and refrigerate for 1 hour.

3 For the tomato toasts: preheat oven to 200°C (400°F, gas mark 6). Using a 5 cm pastry cutter, cut out 4 rounds from each slice of the chilled sandwich bread. Combine garlic and oil.

Brush a baking tray with half the garlic oil, place the rounds on baking tray and brush with remaining oil. Cook for 10 minutes or until golden. Cool, and spread with pesto and top with mozzarella, tomatoes and olives. Season with pepper and serve.

4 For the salmon rounds: cut out 3 rounds from each slice of chilled rye bread with a 5 cm pastry cutter and brush with softened butter. Combine salmon, lemon juice, fromage frais, horseradish and seasoning in a small bowl. Spoon a small amount onto each round and serve.

smoked trout rillettes

ingredients

240 g (7½ oz) smoked trout fillets
finely grated rind (zest) and juice of
1 lemon
2 tablespoons dry sherry
3 tablespoons butter, softened
extra 3 tablespoons butter, melted, for
sealing (optional)
1 teaspoon capers, drained and chopped
extra capers to garnish (optional)
fresh herbs to garnish (optional)
serves 4

i

preparation time
15 minutes, plus
30 minutes
refrigeration

cooking time
10 minutes

**nutritional value
per serve**
fat: 14.9 g
carbohydrate: 0.7 g
protein: 15.4 g

1 Into a large bowl, flake the fish, add lemon rind and juice, sherry, softened butter and capers, mixing well to combine. Alternatively, use a food processor or blender.

2 Spoon mixture into small bowls or ramekins. Pour over the melted butter, if using, and garnish with the herbs or capers, if using. Cover and refrigerate for 30 minutes or until the butter has set.

creamy chickpea and tomato dip

ingredients

250 g (8 oz) dried chickpeas
1/2 cup (125 ml, 4 fl oz) olive oil,
   plus extra for drizzling (optional)
finely grated rind (zest) of 1/2 lemon
juice of 2 lemons
360 g (12 oz) plum tomatoes
2 cloves garlic, crushed
2 spring onions (green onions),
   finely chopped (optional)
3 tablespoons finely chopped
   fresh parsley
salt and black pepper

serves 6

1 Soak the chickpeas in cold water for 12 hours, or overnight. Drain and rinse thoroughly, then place in a large pan and cover with fresh water. Bring to the boil and cook for 10 minutes, removing any foam with a slotted spoon. Reduce heat and simmer, covered, for 1 hour or until tender.

2 Drain the chickpeas, reserving 1/2 cup (125 ml, 4 fl oz) of the cooking liquid, and set a few aside to garnish. In a food processor blend the remaining chickpeas to a fairly smooth paste, along with the reserved cooking liquid, oil and lemon juice. Transfer to a bowl.

3 In a large bowl, place tomatoes and cover with boiling water. Leave for 30 seconds, peel, deseed and roughly chop. Add tomatoes to the chickpea purée along with garlic, lemon rind, spring onions, if using, parsley and seasoning.

4 Mix well and refrigerate for 30 minutes. Before serving, garnish with the reserved chickpeas and drizzle with olive oil, if desired.

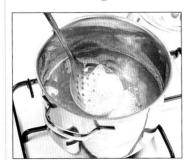

preparation time
15 minutes, plus
12 hours soaking
and 30 minutes
chilling

cooking time
1 hour 15 minutes

**nutritional value
per serve**
fat: 13.7 g
carbohydrate: 5.9 g
protein: 2.8 g

tzatziki

preparation time
15 minutes

nutritional value
per serve
fat: 4.3 g
carbohydrate: 6.5 g
protein: 3.7 g

ingredients

³/₄ cup (185 g, 6 oz) plain greek yoghurt
90 g (3 oz) grated cucumber
1 tablespoon lemon juice
1 clove garlic, crushed
salt and black pepper
1 tablespoon chopped fresh mint
makes 1 cup (250 ml, 8 fl oz)

1 In a large bowl, combine all ingredients, and season with salt and pepper to taste. Cover and refrigerate for at least 1 hour (to allow the flavours to develop).

2 Serve with pita bread as a dip, or as an accompaniment sauce.

roasted eggplant and garlic dip

ingredients

1 large eggplant (aubergine)
5 cloves garlic, roasted
1 tablespoon tahini (sesame paste)
1 tablespoon lemon juice
1 tablespoon olive oil
salt and black pepper
makes 2 cups (500 ml, 16 fl oz)

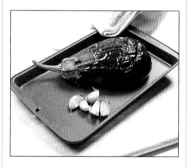

1 Pre-heat the oven to 200°C (400°F, gas mark 6).

2 Place the eggplant and garlic on a baking tray, drizzle with olive oil and roast in the oven for 20 minutes.

preparation time
15 minutes, plus
30 minutes
refrigeration

cooking time
20 minutes

nutritional value
per serve
fat: 9.9 g
carbohydrate: 3 g
protein: 2.7 g

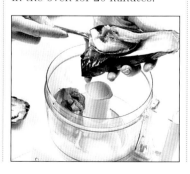

Remove from oven, scoop out flesh from eggplant and place the flesh and roasted garlic in a food processor.

3 Process until smooth, add tahini, lemon juice and olive oil, and process for a further few seconds to combine.

4 Season to taste and serve with bread.

taramo-salata

ingredients

4 slices stale white bread
90 g (3 oz) taramosalata (fish roe, red caviar)
³/₄ cup (185 ml, 6 fl oz) vegetable oil
³/₄ cup (185 ml, 6 fl oz) olive oil
juice of 1 lemon
1 tablespoon water
1 tablespoon chopped fresh mint
makes 600 ml (1 pint)

preparation time
5 minutes

cooking time
10 minutes

nutritional value per serve
fat: 60.8 g
carbohydrate: 7.9 g
protein: 4.5 g

1 Remove crusts from bread and soak the bread in water for 10 minutes. Squeeze all excess water from bread and place in food processor. Process for 30 seconds. Add the taramosalata and process for a further 30 seconds.

2 With the processor still running, pour the oil in a continuous stream until all the oil has been added and the mixture is creamy and thick.

3 Add lemon juice and water and process until well combined. Remove, place in a bowl, and store in the refrigerator for up to 7 days.

4 Serve with toasted pita bread.

breadsticks wrapped in parma ham and rocket

2 Tightly wrap the ham around the breadstick, tucking it in neatly at the top. Brush ham with the remaining oil. Serve.

ingredients

15 g (½ oz) pack rocket
3 tablespoons olive oil
6 thin slices parma ham
6 breadsticks
makes 6

preparation time
5 minutes

nutritional value per serve
fat: 25.4 g
carbohydrate: 16.4 g
protein: 1.8 g

1 Brush rocket or basil leaves with a little oil. Place a few leaves in the middle of each ham slice, then place a breadstick in the centre, leaving about 7.5 cm uncovered to use as a handle.

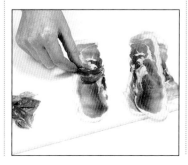

1 Preheat grill to high. Stretch each bacon rasher with the back of a knife, then cut into 3 pieces. Place 2 walnut halves inside each apricot and wrap a piece of bacon around it. Secure with a moistened tooth pick.

2 Grill the wrapped apricots for 2 minutes each side until crisp and golden. Serve

apricots with walnuts and bacon

ingredients

2 slices rindless bacon
12 walnut halves
6 dried apricots
serves 6

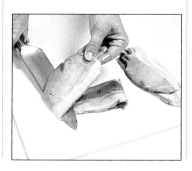

preparation time
5 minutes

cooking time
5 minutes

nutritional value per serve
fat: 20.5 g
carbohydrate: 7.6 g
protein: 16.7 g

sweet capsicum terrine with basil vinaigrette

ingredients

butter for greasing
2 red capsicums (peppers), halved and
  deseeded
2 yellow capsicums, halved and
  deseeded
3 tablespoons olive oil
1 red chilli, deseeded and thinly sliced
250 g (8 oz) ricotta cheese
125 g (4 oz) mature cheddar cheese,
  grated
1 tablespoon dijon mustard
1 teaspoon salt
3 medium eggs, beaten
basil vinaigrette
2 tablespoons white-wine vinegar
2 tablespoons extra virgin olive oil
4 tablespoons sunflower oil
2 spring onions (green onions),
  finely sliced
3 tablespoons finely chopped fresh basil
salt and black pepper
serves 6

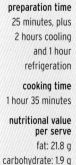

preparation time
25 minutes, plus
2 hours cooling
and 1 hour
refrigeration

cooking time
1 hour 35 minutes

**nutritional value
per serve**
fat: 21.8 g
carbohydrate: 1.9 g
protein: 7.3 g

1 Preheat oven to 190°C (375°F, gas mark 5). Butter a large sheet of baking paper and line a 450 g (14 oz) loaf tin, leaving enough paper to cover the top. Finely dice half a red and half a yellow capsicum and set aside. Roughly chop the rest. Set aside.

2 Heat oil in a large heavy-based pan, add the

chopped capsicums and chilli, then cook, covered, for 20 minutes or until softened. Purée in a food processor, then press through a sieve. In a large bowl combine the ricotta, cheddar, mustard, salt and eggs, then stir in the purée and diced capsicums. Pour into the tin, then fold paper over to cover the terrine without touching. Place in a roasting tin.

3 Pour in enough boiling water to reach halfway up the sides of the loaf tin, then cook for 1 hour 15 minutes, adding more water if necessary. Cool for 2 hours, then refrigerate for 1 hour. Invert onto a plate and peel off the paper. To make the vinaigrette, combine all ingredients in a small bowl, whisking well to combine. Serve sliced terrine drizzled with vinaigrette and crusty bread or toast.

1 Combine dressing ingredients in a jar and shake well.

2 Place the scallops on a plate suitable for steaming. Sprinkle scallops with a little of the dressing and steam gently over boiling water for 6 minutes.

3 Snap watercress into 10 cm sections. In a large serving bowl, combine watercress, water chestnuts, cherry tomatoes, walnuts and bean shoots. Pour over the dressing and toss gently to coat well. Gently mix in the scallops and serve.

scallop and watercress salad

ingredients

10 fresh scallops
90 g (3 oz) watercress; discard woody stems, select tender tips only
160 g (5½ oz) water chestnuts, halved
4 cherry tomatoes
50 g (1¾ oz) walnut halves
90 g (3 oz) bean shoots

dressing

⅔ cup (170 ml, 5½ fl oz) walnut or olive oil
2 tablespoons red-wine vinegar
2 small cloves garlic, crushed
salt and white pepper

serves 4

preparation time
25 minutes, plus 2 hours cooling and 1 hour refrigeration

cooking time
1 hour 35 minutes

nutritional value per serve
fat: 24.2 g
carbohydrate: 2.8 g
protein: 3.7 g

anchovy, egg and parmesan salad

ingredients

3 medium eggs
2 heads endive (chicory)
2 small butter lettuces, leaves torn
12 anchovy fillets in oil, drained and cut
   in half lengthways
1 tablespoon capers, drained
3 cherry tomatoes, halved
50 g (1³/₄ oz) parmesan cheese
3 tablespoons extra virgin olive oil
juice of 1 lemon
salt and black pepper
fresh flat-leaf parsley to garnish
serves 6

1 Bring a small pan of water to the boil, add eggs and boil for 10 minutes. Remove from pan, cool under cold running water, then shell. Cut each egg lengthways into quarters.

2 On each serving plate, arrange 8 alternating endive and lettuce leaves, tips facing outwards, in a star shape. Place 2 egg quarters on the base of 2 opposite lettuce leaves, then place 2 anchovy halves on the other 2 opposite lettuce leaves. Scatter the capers over the leaves.

3 Put a cherry tomato half in the centre of each plate and drape 2 anchovy halves over the top. Shave over the parmesan, using a vegetable peeler, then drizzle over the olive oil and lemon juice. Season to taste and garnish with parsley.

preparation time
10 minutes

cooking time
10 minutes

nutritional value per serve
fat: 5.0 g
carbohydrate: 0.6 g
protein: 3.7 g

starters
hot

broccoli soufflés with olive purée

ingredients

butter for greasing
450 g (14 oz) broccoli, chopped
280 ml (9 fl oz) pouring cream
4 medium eggs, separated
salt and black pepper
olive purée
20 pitted black olives
½ cup (125 ml, 4 fl oz) olive oil
grated rind (zest) and juice of 1 lemon
serves 4

1 Preheat oven to 220°C (425°F, gas mark 7). Grease 4 individual 1 cup (250 ml, 8 fl oz) capacity ramekin dishes. Cook broccoli in a little boiling water for 10 minutes until tender, drain well. Process to a smooth purée with the cream, egg yolks and seasoning in a food processor. Transfer to a large mixing bowl.

preparation time
15 minutes

cooking time
40 minutes

nutritional value per serve
fat: 22.1 g
carbohydrate: 2.6 g
protein: 4.5 g

2 Beat egg whites to form soft peaks. Gently fold one-third of the beaten whites into the broccoli purée, using a large metal spoon. Carefully fold in the remaining whites in two batches, mixing well.

3 Divide mixture between ramekin dishes and cook for 20–25 minutes, until risen and golden. Purée olives, olive oil and lemon rind (zest) and juice in a food processor until smooth. Serve with warm soufflés and crusty bread.

mushrooms in wine

ingredients

4 tablespoons olive oil
1 small clove garlic, peeled
750 g (1½ lb) mushrooms, sliced
1 tablespoon chopped fresh thyme
salt
freshly ground black pepper
½ cup (125 ml, 4 fl oz) white wine
2 tablespoons chopped fresh parsley
serves 4-6

1 Heat oil and garlic in a large pan over high heat, add mushrooms and thyme and cook, stirring, for 1–2 minutes. Season to taste, add wine and bring to the boil. Boil rapidly until wine is almost evaporated. Transfer to a serving bowl, sprinkle with parsley and serve hot or cold.

preparation time
10 minutes

cooking time
25 minutes

**nutritional value
per serve**
fat: 7.8 g
carbohydrate: 1.3 g
protein: 2.9 g

tomato toasts with fresh basil

ingredients

4 tablespoons olive oil
½ teaspoon mixed dried herbs
black pepper
1 long bread stick (baguette), cut into
   12 slices
8 plum tomatoes
1 clove garlic, crushed
30 g (1 oz) sun-dried tomatoes in oil,
   drained and finely chopped
1 teaspoon vinegar
1 teaspoon sugar
2 tablespoons chopped fresh basil
serves 4

preparation time
10 minutes

cooking time
15 minutes

nutritional value
per serve
fat: 8.6 g
carbohydrate: 25.2 g
protein: 4.7 g

1 Preheat oven to 220°C (425°F, gas mark 7). Combine 3 tablespoons of the oil with the dried herbs and season well. Brush both sides of each bread slice with the flavoured oil. Cook for 8 minutes or until lightly golden and crisp.

2 In a large bowl, place tomatoes and cover with boiling water. Leave for 30 seconds. Peel and deseed, then roughly chop the flesh. Set aside.

3 Heat the remaining olive oil in a large frying pan, add garlic, chopped tomatoes, sun-dried tomatoes, vinegar, sugar and basil. Cook, stirring occasionally, for 5 minutes or until heated through. Remove from heat. Spoon tomato mixture onto each of toasts, season and serve.

mixed mushroom frittata

ingredients

4 eggs, lightly beaten
½ cup (125 ml, 4 fl oz) milk
1 tablespoon dijon mustard
2 tablespoons chopped fresh dill
freshly ground black pepper
cooking spray
4 spring onions (green onions),
  chopped
125 g (4 oz) oyster mushrooms
125 g (4 oz) field mushrooms, sliced
125 g (4 oz) button mushrooms, sliced
serves 4

preparation time
25 minutes

cooking time
25 minutes

**nutritional value
per serve**
fat: 3.1 g
carbohydrate: 1.9 g
protein: 5.2 g

1 In a large bowl, place eggs, milk, mustard, dill and black pepper to taste and whisk to combine.

2 Heat a large non-stick frying pan over a medium heat. Coat with cooking spray, add spring onions and cook, stirring, for 2 minutes. Add mushrooms and cook, stirring for a further 3 minutes or until mushrooms are tender.

3 Pour egg mixture into pan and cook over a low heat for 5–10 minutes or until frittata is almost set. Preheat grill to medium.

4 Place pan under grill and cook for 3 minutes or until top is golden.

spicy deep-fried calamari rings

ingredients

60 g (2 oz) plain flour
2 tablespoons paprika
1 teaspoon salt
500 g (1 lb) fresh calamari (squid),
   cut into rings
vegetable oil for deep-frying

serves 4

preparation time
10 minutes,
2 hours marinating

cooking time
10 minutes

**nutritional value
per serve**
fat: 17.9 g
carbohydrate: 6.3 g
protein: 13.2 g

1 In a large bowl, combine flour, paprika and salt. Toss the calamari rings in the seasoned flour to coat evenly. Set aside.

2 Heat 5 cm of vegetable oil in a large heavy-based pan. Test that the oil is ready by adding a calamari ring – it should sizzle at once. Cook a quarter of the rings for 1–2 minutes, until golden. Drain on kitchen towels and keep warm while you cook the remaining rings in 3 more batches.

grilled oysters with champagne and cream

ingredients

12 fresh oysters (in shell)
3 tablespoons champagne, dry
   sparkling wine or dry vermouth
2 tablespoons butter
2 tablespoons double cream
black pepper
125 g (4 oz) baby spinach
serves 4

1 To open each oyster, place a thick cloth on a work surface and put the shell on top, flat side up. Wrap a cloth round your hand and insert a small sharp knife between the halves opposite the hinge. Carefully work the knife back and forth to loosen the muscle attached to the inside of the flat shell, then prise open. Scoop out each oyster with a teaspoon and strain the juices into a small pan. Remove and discard the muscle from the 12 rounded half-shells, then wash and dry. Place in an ovenproof dish lined with crumpled foil so shells sit level.

2 Bring the juices to a simmer and poach the oysters for 30–60 seconds, until just firm. Remove from pan. Add champagne to the pan and boil for 2 minutes to reduce. Remove from heat and whisk in butter, then cream. Season with pepper.

3 Preheat the grill to high. Cook the spinach in a small pan of boiling water for 1–2 minutes, until wilted. Squeeze out excess liquid and divide between the shells. Top with an oyster and spoon over a little sauce. Grill for 1 minute or until heated through.

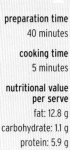

preparation time
40 minutes

cooking time
5 minutes

**nutritional value
per serve**
fat: 12.8 g
carbohydrate: 1.1 g
protein: 5.9 g

thai fish cakes

ingredients

500 g (1 lb) boneless firm white fish
   fillets, skinned
3 spring onions (green onions),
   chopped
1 egg, lightly beaten
2 tablespoons plain flour
2 fresh red chillies, deseeded and
   chopped
1/2 teaspoon cumin seeds
2 teaspoons grated fresh ginger
vegetable oil for shallow-frying
coriander chutney
1 bunch fresh coriander
4 spring onions (green onions),
   chopped
1 tablespoon grated fresh ginger
1 clove garlic, crushed
2 tablespoons lime or lemon juice
1 tablespoon vegetable oil
serves 4-6

preparation time
25 minutes

cooking time
10 minutes

nutritional value
fat: 14.7 g
carbohydrate: 2.5 g
protein: 11.3 g

1 Place fish in a food
processor and process until
finely chopped. Add spring
onions, egg, flour, chillies,
cumin seeds and ginger and
process to make a stiff paste.

2 Take 2 tablespoons of fish
mixture and shape into a
small flat cake. Place on a
plate lined with plastic food
wrap. Repeat with remaining
mixture.

3 Heat oil in a frying pan over
a medium heat and cook
fish cakes in batches for 3–4
minutes each side or until
cooked. Set aside and keep
warm.

4 For the chutney: place
coriander, spring onions,
ginger, garlic, lime or lemon
juice and oil in a food
processor and process until
smooth. Serve warm with fish
cakes.

nut-crusted fish bites

ingredients

50 g (1³/₄ oz) hazelnuts, chopped
60 g (2 oz) fresh breadcrumbs
30 g (1 oz) plain flour
salt and black pepper
1 large egg, beaten
500 g (1 lb) firm white fish fillet, cut
   into 20 even-sized pieces
vegetable oil for shallow frying
tartare sauce, vinegar or lemon juice
   to serve
serves 4

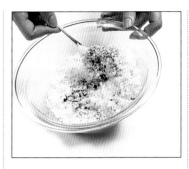

1 In a large shallow bowl, combine the nuts and breadcrumbs. Place flour into another bowl and season. Place egg into a third bowl. Dip the fish pieces into flour, then egg and finally the breadcrumb mixture to coat. Set aside.

2 Heat 1 cm of oil in a large frying pan and fry fish pieces in batches for 5 minutes or until golden on all sides. Drain on kitchen towels and keep warm. Serve with tartare sauce or sprinkled with vinegar or lemon juice.

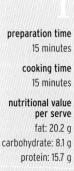

preparation time
15 minutes

cooking time
15 minutes

**nutritional value
per serve**
fat: 20.2 g
carbohydrate: 8.1 g
protein: 15.7 g

potato cakes with smoked salmon

ingredients

300 g (10 oz) floury potatoes, unpeeled
150 ml (5 fl oz) milk
salt and black pepper
1 large egg
30 g (1 oz) plain flour
4 spring onions (green onions), finely
   sliced
1 tablespoon oil
$^{1}/_{2}$ cup (125 ml, 4 fl oz) crème fraîche
2 tablespoons chopped fresh dill
150 g (5 oz) smoked salmon slices
extra dill to garnish
lemon wedges to serve
serves 4

1 Cook the potatoes in boiling salted water for 15–20 minutes, until tender, drain. Cool for a few minutes, then peel. Mash with milk, season, then beat in the egg, flour and spring onions to make a batter.

2 Heat a large non-stick frying pan, add a little of the oil. Make 4 potato cakes, using 2 tablespoons of batter for each. Fry for 2–3 minutes on each side until golden. Drain on kitchen towels and keep warm while you make 2 further batches of 4 potato cakes.

3 Combine the crème fraîche and chopped dill. Serve pancakes topped with the salmon slices and a spoonful of crème fraîche. Garnish with black pepper, dill and lemon.

preparation time
15 minutes

cooking time
40 minutes

**nutritional value
per serve**
fat: 7.9 g
carbohydrate: 8.5 g
protein: 6.9 g

glamorgan sausages with tomato salad

ingredients

100 g (3¹/₂ oz) potato
100 g (3¹/₂ oz) white breadcrumbs
150 g (5 oz) mature cheddar cheese, grated
1 small leek, finely chopped
¹/₄ teaspoon dried sage
1 tablespoon chopped fresh parsley
salt and black pepper
pinch cayenne pepper
2 egg yolks
3 tablespoons plain flour
1 medium egg, beaten
oil for shallow frying

salad

3 tablespoons olive oil
2 teaspoons balsamic vinegar
pinch brown sugar
150 g (5 oz) cherry tomatoes, halved
1 red onion, thinly sliced
5 cm piece cucumber, sliced
fresh basil leaves

preparation time
20 minutes, plus 15 minutes cooling and 1 hour refrigeration

cooking time
35 minutes

nutritional value per serve
fat: 23.2 g
carbohydrate: 11.6 g
protein: 7.2 g

1 Cook the potato in boiling salted water for 15–20 minutes, until tender. Drain well, mash, then leave to cool for 15 minutes. Mix the cold mash with half the breadcrumbs, the cheese, leek, sage and parsley. Season with salt, pepper and cayenne. Add egg yolks and combine well. Using your hands, shape into 12 sausages. Cover and refrigerate for 1 hour.

2 Season the flour and place in a shallow dish. Place beaten egg in a bowl. Dip the sausages into the seasoned flour, then into the beaten egg, then coat in the remaining breadcrumbs. Heat 5 mm of oil in a large frying pan and fry half the sausages, turning, for 10 minutes or until golden brown. Drain on kitchen towels and keep warm while you cook the remaining sausages.

3 In a large bowl whisk together the oil, vinegar and sugar. Add tomatoes, onion, cucumber and basil and toss well to coast. Season and serve with the sausages.

beef carpaccio

ingredients

450 g (14 oz) beef fillet, sliced into
    4 mm slices
125 g (4 oz) rocket (arugula), washed
1 tablespoon balsamic vinegar
3 tablespoons extra virgin olive oil
pecorino cheese shavings
freshly ground black pepper
salt

serves 6

preparation time
15-20 minutes

nutritional value
fat: 12.4 g
carbohydrate: 0.5 g
protein: 15.5 g

1 Lightly oil a sheet of greaseproof paper and season lightly.

2 Arrange 4 slices of beef on paper approximately 5 cm apart. Place another oiled piece of greaseproof paper on top, and gently beat the meat, until it has spread out to at least twice its former size. Repeat with remaining meat slices.

3 Refrigerate until needed. Alternatively, partly freeze the meat, (before slicing thinly).

4 Place some rocket in the centre of a serving plate, arrange beef slices around the rocket, and drizzle with some balsamic vinegar and olive oil. Serve with pecorino shavings and black pepper.

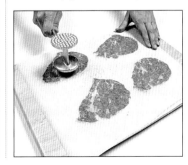

smoked salmon soufflés

ingredients

45 g (1½ oz) parmesan cheese
1 tablespoon butter
2 tablespoons plain flour
½ cup (125 ml, 4 fl oz) milk
4 tablespoons double cream
3 eggs, separated
60 g (2 oz) gruyère cheese, grated
60 g (2 oz) smoked salmon, shredded
1 tablespoon chopped fresh dill
serves 2

1 Grease 2 ramekins of 1 cup (250 ml, 8 fl oz) capacity and sprinkle base and sides with 30 g (1 oz) parmesan cheese.

2 Melt butter in a small pan over a medium heat. Stir in flour and cook for 2 minutes. Remove pan from heat and gradually whisk in milk and cream.

3 Return pan to heat and cook, stirring constantly, for 4 minutes or until sauce boils and thickens. Remove pan from heat and set aside to cool slightly.

4 Add egg yolks, gruyère cheese, remaining parmesan cheese, salmon and dill to sauce and mix to combine.

5 In a large bowl, place egg whites and beat until stiff peaks form. Fold egg white mixture into salmon mixture. Pour into ramekins and bake for 20–25 minutes or until soufflés are puffed and golden. Serve immediately.

preparation time
15 minutes

cooking time
35 minutes

nutritional value
fat: 20.4 g
carbohydrate: 3.1 g
protein: 13.4 g

glossary

al dente: Italian term to describe pasta and rice that are cooked until tender but still firm to the bite.

bake blind: to bake pastry cases without their fillings. Line the raw pastry case with greaseproof paper and fill with raw rice or dried beans to prevent collapsed sides and puffed base. Remove paper and fill 5 minutes before completion of cooking time.

baste: to spoon hot cooking liquid over food at intervals during cooking to moisten and flavour it.

beat: to make a mixture smooth with rapid and regular motions using a spatula, wire whisk or electric mixer; to make a mixture light and smooth by enclosing air.

beurre manié: equal quantities of butter and flour mixed together to a smooth paste and stirred bit by bit into a soup, stew or sauce while on the heat to thicken. Stop adding when desired thickness results.

bind: to add egg or a thick sauce to hold ingredients together when cooked.

blanch: to plunge some foods into boiling water for less than a minute and immediately plunge into iced water. This is to brighten the colour of some vegetables; to remove skin from tomatoes and nuts.

blend: to mix 2 or more ingredients thoroughly together; do not confuse with blending in an electric blender.

boil: to cook in a liquid brought to boiling point and kept there.

boiling point: when bubbles rise continually and break over the entire surface of the liquid, reaching a temperature of 100°C (212°F). In some cases food is held at this high temperature for a few seconds then heat is turned to low for slower cooking. See simmer.

bouquet garni: a bundle of several herbs tied together with string for easy removal, placed into pots of stock, soups and stews for flavour. A few sprigs of fresh thyme, parsley and bay leaf are used. Can be purchased in sachet form for convenience.

caramelise: to heat sugar in a heavy-based pan until it liquefies and develops a caramel colour. Vegetables such as blanched carrots and sautéed onions may be sprinkled with sugar and caramelised.

chill: to place in the refrigerator or stir over ice until cold.

clarify: to make a liquid clear by removing sediments and impurities. To melt fat and remove any sediment.

coat: to dust or roll food items in flour to cover the surface before the food is cooked. Also, to coat in flour, egg and breadcrumbs.

cool: to stand at room temperature until some or all heat is removed, eg, cool a little, cool completely.

cream: to make creamy and fluffy by working the mixture with the back of a wooden spoon, usually refers to creaming butter and sugar or margarine. May also be creamed with an electric mixer.

croutons: small cubes of bread, toasted or fried, used as an addition to salads or as a garnish to soups and stews.

crudite: raw vegetable sticks served with a dipping sauce.

crumb: to coat foods in flour, egg and breadcrumbs to form a protective coating for foods which are fried. Also adds flavour, texture and enhances appearance.

cube: to cut into small pieces with six even sides, eg, cubes of meat.

cut in: to combine fat and flour using 2 knives scissor fashion or with a pastry blender, to make pastry.

deglaze: to dissolve dried out cooking juices left on the base and sides of a roasting dish or frying pan. Add a little water, wine or stock, scrape and stir over heat until dissolved. Resulting liquid is used to make a flavoursome gravy or added to a sauce or casserole.

degrease: to skim fat from the surface of cooking liquids, eg, stocks, soups, casseroles.

dice: to cut into small cubes.

dredge: to heavily coat with icing sugar, sugar, flour or cornflour.

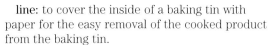

dressing: a mixture added to completed dishes to add moisture and flavour, eg, salads, cooked vegetables.

drizzle: to pour in a fine thread-like stream moving over a surface.

egg wash: beaten egg with milk or water used to brush over pastry, bread dough or biscuits to give a sheen and golden brown colour.

essence: a strong flavouring liquid, usually made by distillation. Only a few drops are needed to flavour.

fillet: a piece of prime meat, fish or poultry which is boneless or has all bones removed.

flake: to separate cooked fish into flakes, removing any bones and skin, using 2 forks.

flame: to ignite warmed alcohol over food or to pour into a pan with food, ignite then serve.

flute: to make decorative indentations around the pastry rim before baking.

fold in: combining of a light, whisked or creamed mixture with other ingredients. Add a portion of the other ingredients at a time and mix using a gentle circular motion, over and under the mixture so that air will not be lost. Use a silver spoon or spatula.

glaze: to brush or coat food with a liquid that will give the finished product a glossy appearance, and on baked products, a golden brown colour.

grease: to rub the surface of a metal or heatproof dish with oil or fat, to prevent the food from sticking.

herbed butter: softened butter mixed with finely chopped fresh herbs and re-chilled. Used to serve on grilled meats and fish.

hors d'ouvre: small savoury foods served as an appetiser, popularly known today as 'finger food'.

infuse: to steep foods in a liquid until the liquid absorbs their flavour.

joint: to cut poultry and game into serving pieces by dividing at the joint.

julienne: to cut some food, eg, vegetables and processed meats into fine strips the length of matchsticks. Used for inclusion in salads or as a garnish to cooked dishes.

knead: to work a yeast dough in a pressing, stretching and folding motion with the heel of the hand until smooth and elastic to develop the gluten strands. Non-yeast doughs should be lightly and quickly handled as gluten development is not desired.

line: to cover the inside of a baking tin with paper for the easy removal of the cooked product from the baking tin.

macerate: to stand fruit in a syrup, liqueur or spirit to give added flavour.

marinade: a flavoured liquid, into which food is placed for some time to give it flavour and to tenderise. Marinades include an acid ingredient such as vinegar or wine, oil and seasonings.

mask: to evenly cover cooked food portions with a sauce, mayonnaise or savoury jelly.

pan-fry: to fry foods in a small amount of fat or oil, sufficient to coat the base of the pan.

parboil: to boil until partially cooked. The food is then finished by some other method.

pare: to peel the skin from vegetables and fruit. Peel is the popular term but pare is the name given to the knife used; paring knife.

pith: the white lining between the rind and flesh of oranges, grapefruit and lemons.

pit: to remove stones or seeds from olives, cherries, dates.

pitted: the olives, cherries, dates etc, with the stone removed, eg, purchase pitted dates.

poach: to simmer gently in enough hot liquid to almost cover the food so shape will be retained.

pound: to flatten meats with a meat mallet; to reduce to a paste or small particles with a mortar and pestle.

simmer: to cook in liquid just below boiling point at about 96°C (205°F) with small bubbles rising gently to the surface.

skim: to remove fat or froth from the surface of simmering food.

stock: the liquid produced when meat, poultry, fish or vegetables have been simmered in water to extract the flavour. Used as a base for soups, sauces, casseroles etc. Convenience stock products are available.

sweat: to cook sliced onions or vegetables, in a small amount of butter in a covered pan over low heat, to soften them and release flavour without colouring.

conversions

measurements differ from country to country, so it's important to understand what the differences are. This Measurements Guide gives you simple 'at-a-glance' information for using the recipes in this book, wherever you may be.

Cooking is not an exact science – minor variations in measurements won't make a difference to your cooking.

equipment

There is a difference in the size of measuring cups used internationally, but the difference is minimal (only 2–3 teaspoons). We use the Australian standard metric measurements in our recipes:

1 teaspoon ....5 ml   1 tablespoon....20 ml
1/2 cup......125 ml   1 cup.....250 ml
4 cups...1 litre

Measuring cups come in sets of one cup (250 ml), 1/2 cup (125 ml), 1/3 cup (80 ml) and 1/4 cup (60 ml). Use these for measuring liquids and certain dry ingredients.

Measuring spoons come in a set of four and should be used for measuring dry and liquid ingredients.

When using cup or spoon measures always make them level (unless the recipe indicates otherwise).

dry versus wet ingredients

While this system of measures is consistent for liquids, it's more difficult to quantify dry ingredients. For instance, one level cup equals: 200 g of brown sugar; 210 g of castor sugar; and 110 g of icing sugar.

When measuring dry ingredients such as flour, don't push the flour down or shake it into the cup. It is best just to spoon the flour in until it reaches the desired amount. When measuring liquids use a clear vessel indicating metric levels.

Always use medium eggs (55–60 g) when eggs are required in a recipe.

dry

metric (grams)	imperial (ounces)
30 g	1 oz
60 g	2 oz
90 g	3 oz
100 g	3 1/2 oz
125 g	4 oz
150 g	5 oz
185 g	6 oz
200 g	7 oz
250 g	8 oz
280 g	9 oz
315 g	10 oz
330 g	11 oz
370 g	12 oz
400 g	13 oz
440 g	14 oz
470 g	15 oz
500 g	16 oz (1 lb)
750 g	24 oz (1 1/2 lb)
1000 g (1 kg)	32 oz (2 lb)

liquids

metric (millilitres)	imperial (fluid ounces)
30 ml	1 fl oz
60 ml	2 fl oz
90 ml	3 fl oz
100 ml	3 1/2 fl oz
125 ml	4 fl oz
150 ml	5 fl oz
190 ml	6 fl oz
250 ml	8 fl oz
300 ml	10 fl oz
500 ml	16 fl oz
600 ml	20 fl oz (1 pint)*
1000 ml (1 litre)	32 fl oz

*Note: an American pint is 16 fl oz.

oven
Your oven should always be at the right temperature before placing the food in it to be cooked. Note that if your oven doesn't have a fan you may need to cook food for a little longer.

microwave
It is difficult to give an exact cooking time for microwave cooking. It is best to watch what you are cooking closely to monitor its progress.

standing time
Many foods continue to cook when you take them out of the oven or microwave. If a recipe states that the food needs to 'stand' after cooking, be sure not to overcook the dish.

can sizes

The can sizes available in your supermarket or grocery store may not be the same as specified in the recipe. Don't worry if there is a small variation in size—it's unlikely to make a difference to the end result.

cooking temperatures	°C (celsius)	°F (fahrenheit)	gas mark
very slow	120	250	1/2
slow	150	300	2
moderately slow	160	315	2-3
moderate	180	350	4
moderate hot	190	375	5
	200	400	6
hot	220	425	7
very hot	230	450	8
	240	475	9
	250	500	10

index